More about *HOW TO LOVE A COUNTRY*:

"Richard Blanco has risen to the challenge of writing poetry that serves our nation. This is both a responsibility and an honor. I am moved, proud, overjoyed, and inspired."

—SANDRA CISNEROS,
author of *House on Mango Street*

"Powerful, personal, and full of life, these poems delve into the complex intricacies of what it means to call the United States home. A masterful poet who is clear-eyed and full of heart, Blanco explores the country's haunted past while offering a bright hope for the future."

—ADA LIMÓN,
author of *Bright Dead Things*

"In this timely collection, Richard Blanco masterfully embraces his role as a civic poet, confronting our nation's riddled history in the light of conscience. At once personal and political, these lyric narratives decry injustice and proclaim our hopes."

—CAROLYN FORCHÉ,
author of *The Country Between Us*

"There is a uniting oneness to these passionate and remarkable poems, each finely wrought line a bridge from one heart to another, a love song of this burdened earth and all its flawed inhabitants. Richard Blanco is this century's Walt Whitman."

—ANDRE DUBUS III,
author of *Gone So Long*

HOW TO

LOVE A COUNTRY

HOW TO LOVE A COUNTRY

Poems

Richard Blanco

Beacon Press • *Boston*

BEACON PRESS
Boston, Massachusetts
www.beacon.org

Beacon Press books
are published under the auspices of
the Unitarian Universalist Association
of Congregations.

22 21 20 19   8 7 6 5 4 3 2 1

LIBRARY OF CONGRESS CATALOGING-IN-PUBLICATION DATA

Names: Blanco, Richard, author.
Title: How to love a country : poems / Richard Blanco.
Description: Boston : Beacon Press, [2019]
Identifiers: LCCN 2018050554 (print) | LCCN 2018054477 (ebook) | ISBN
    9780807025987 (ebook) | ISBN 9780807025918 (hardcover : alk. paper)
Subjects: LCSH: American poetry—21st century.
Classification: LCC PS3552.L36533 (ebook) | LCC PS3552.L36533 A6 2019 (print)
    | DDC 811/.54—dc23
LC record available at https://lccn.loc.gov/2018050554

Text design by Michael Starkman
at Wilsted & Taylor Publishing Services

*Dime con quién andas, y te diré
quién eres.*

*Tell me with whom you walk,
and I'll tell you who you are.*

———

These poems are for all those
whose trailblazing footsteps
I followed here, and for all
those I now walk alongside
with compassion, hope, and the
audacity to believe that someday
all of us will walk together.

I'm both a poet and one of the "everybodies" of my country. I live with manipulated fear, ignorance, cultural confusion and social antagonism huddling together on the faultline of an empire.

ADRIENNE RICH

The role of the artist is exactly the same as the role of the lover. If I love you, I have to make you conscious of the things you don't see.

JAMES A. BALDWIN

CONTENTS

I

II

III

HOW TO
LOVE A COUNTRY

DECLARATION OF INTER-DEPENDENCE

Such has been the patient sufferance . . .

We're a mother's bread, instant potatoes, milk at a checkout line. We're her three children pleading for bubble gum and their father. We're the three minutes she steals to page through a tabloid, needing to believe even stars' lives are as joyful and bruised.

Our repeated petitions have been answered only by repeated injury . . .

We're her second job serving an executive absorbed in his *Wall Street Journal* at a sidewalk café shadowed by skyscrapers. We're the shadows of the fortune he won and the family he lost. We're his loss and the lost. We're a father in a coal town who can't mine a life anymore because too much and too little has happened, for too long.

A history of repeated injuries and usurpations . . .

We're the grit of his main street's blacked-out windows and graffitied truths. We're a street in another town lined with royal palms, at home with a Peace Corps couple who collect African art. We're their dinner-party talk of wines, wielded picket signs, and burned draft cards. We're what they know: it's time to do more than read the *New York Times*, buy fair-trade coffee and organic corn.

In every stage of these oppressions we have petitioned for redress . . .

We're the farmer who grew the corn, who plows into his couch as worn as his back by the end of the day. We're his TV set blaring news having everything and nothing to do with the field dust in his eyes or his son nested in the ache of his

1

arms. We're his son. We're a black teenager who drove too fast or too slow, talked too much or too little, moved too quickly, but not quick enough. We're the blast of the bullet leaving the gun. We're the guilt and the grief of the cop who wished he hadn't shot.

We mutually pledge to each other our lives, our fortunes and our sacred honor . . .

We're the dead, we're the living amid the flicker of vigil candlelight. We're in a dim cell with an inmate reading Dostoevsky. We're his crime, his sentence, his amends, we're the mending of ourselves and others. We're a Buddhist serving soup at a shelter alongside a stockbroker. We're each other's shelter and hope: a widow's fifty cents in a collection plate and a golfer's ten-thousand-dollar pledge for a cure.

We hold these truths to be self-evident . . .

We're the cure for hatred caused by despair. We're the good morning of a bus driver who remembers our name, the tattooed man who gives up his seat on the subway. We're every door held open with a smile when we look into each other's eyes the way we behold the moon. We're the moon. We're the promise of one people, one breath declaring to one another: *I see you. I need you. I am you.*

I

ELECTION YEAR

The last ghostly patch of snow slips away,
winter's peaceful abandon slowly melting
into memory and you remember the muck
outside your kitchen window is the garden
you promised to keep, must struggle with
once more. Jeans dyed black by years of dirt,
you step again into the ache of your boots,
clear dead spoils, trowel the soil for new life.

. . .

April's sun shifts on the horizon, lights up
the dewed spiderwebs like chandeliers.
Clouds begin sailing in, cargoed with rain
loud enough to rouse the flowers into
a race for color: the rouged tulips clash
with the lilies flaunting their noble petals
at the brazen puffs of allium, the mauve
tongues of iris gossip sweet-nothings
to the wind trembling through petunias.

. . .

Mornings over coffee and news of the world,
you catch the magic act of hummingbirds—
appearing, disappearing—the eye tricked
into seeing how the garden flowers thrive
in shared soil, drink from the same rainfall,
governed by one sun, yet grow divided
in their beds where they've lain for years.
In the ruts between bands of color, ragweeds
poke their dastard heads, dandelions cough
their poison seeds, and thistles like daggers
draw their spiny leaves and take hold.

. . .

The garden loses ground all summer, calls
you to your duty: with worn gloves molded
by the toll of your toil, armed with shears,
you tear weeds, snip head-bowed blooms,
prop their struggling stems. Butterfly wings
wink at you, hinting it's all a ruse, as you rest
on your deck, proud of your calloused palms
and pained knees, trusting all you've done
is true enough to keep the garden abloom.

· · ·

Then, overnight, a vine you've never battled
creeps out of the dark furrows, scales
the long necks of the sunflowers, chokes
every black-eyed Susan, and coils around
the peonies, beheading them all. You snap
apart its greedy tendrils, cast your hands
back into the dirt, pull at its ruthless roots.
Yet it returns with equal fury, equal claim:
the poppies scream red, the blue asters
gasp for air, strangled in its vile clasp
that lives by killing everything it touches.

· · ·

Fall opens with the sun's eye closing earlier
beyond the mountains, and you lose sleep,
uncertain if the garden you cherish will survive
despite your care. It's not simply the winter
you worry about, but something we call hope
pitted against despair, something we can only
speak of by speaking to ourselves about flowers,
a garden tended under a constitution of stars
we must believe in, splayed across our sky.

DREAMING A WALL

He hates his neighbors' flowers, claims his
are redder, bluer, whiter than theirs, believes
his bees work harder, his soil richer, blacker.
He hears birds sing sweeter in his trees, taller
and fuller, too, but not enough to screen out
the nameless faces next door that he calls
liars, thieves who'd steal his juicier fruit, kill
for his wetter rain and brighter sun. He keeps
a steely eye on them, mocks the too cheery
colors of their homes, too small and too close
to his own, painted white, with room to spare.
He curses the giggles of their children always
barefoot in the yard, chasing their yappy dogs.
He wishes them dead. Closes his blinds. Refuses
to let light from their windows pollute his eyes
with their lives. Denies their silhouettes dining
at the kitchen table, laughing in the living room,
the goodnight kisses through every bedroom.
Slouched in his couch, grumbling over the news
he dismisses as fake, he changes the channel
to an old cowboy western. Amid the clamor
of gunshots he dozes off thinking of his dream
where he stakes a line between him and all
his neighbors, stabs the ground as he would
their chests. Forms a footing cast in blood-red
earth, bends steel bars as he would their bones
with his bare fists and buries them in concrete.
Mortar mixed thick with anger, each brick laid
heavy with revenge, he smiles as he finishes

the last course high enough to imagine them
more miserable and lonely than him alone
behind his wall, worshiping his greener lawn,
praising his fresher air, under his bluer, bluer sky.

COMPLAINT OF EL RÍO GRANDE

for Aylin Barbieri

I was meant for all things to meet:
to make the clouds pause in the mirror
of my waters, to be home to fallen rain
that finds its way to me, to turn eons
of loveless rock into lovesick pebbles
and carry them as humble gifts back
to the sea which brings life back to me.

I felt the sun flare, praised each star
flocked about the moon long before
you did. I've breathed air you'll never
breathe, listened to songbirds before
you could speak their names, before
you dug your oars in me, before you
created the gods that created you.

Then countries—your invention—maps
jigsawing the world into colored shapes
caged in bold lines to say: you're here,
not there, you're this, not that, to say:
yellow isn't red, red isn't black, black is
not white, to say: *mine*, not *ours*, to say
war, and believe life's worth is relative.

You named me big river, drew me—blue,
thick to divide, to say: *spic* and *Yankee*,
to say: *wetback* and *gringo*. You split me

in two—half of me *us*, the rest *them*. But
I wasn't meant to drown children, hear
mothers' cries, never meant to be your
geography: a line, a border, a murderer.

I was meant for all things to meet:
the mirrored clouds and sun's tingle,
birdsongs and the quiet moon, the wind
and its dust, the rush of mountain rain—
and us. Blood that runs in you is water
flowing in me, both life, the truth we
know we know: be one in one another.

COMO TÚ / LIKE YOU / LIKE ME

{for the D.A.C.A. DREAMers and all our nation's immigrants}

> *. . . my veins don't end in me*
> *but in the unanimous blood*
> *of those who struggle for life . . .*
>
> *. . . mis venas no terminan en mí*
> *sino en la sange unánime*
> *de los que luchan por la vida . . .*
>
> —ROQUE DALTON, *Como tú*

Como tú, I question history's blur in my eyes
each time I face a mirror. Like a mirror, I gaze
into my palm a wrinkled map I still can't read,
my lifeline an unnamed road I can't find, can't
trace back to the fork in my parents' trek
that cradled me here. *Como tú*, I woke up to
this dream of a country I didn't choose, that
didn't choose me—trapped in the nightmare
of its hateful glares. *Como tú*, I'm also from
the lakes and farms, waterfalls and prairies
of another country I can't fully claim either.
Como tú, I am either a mirage living among
these faces and streets that raised me here,
or I'm nothing, a memory forgotten by all
I was taken from and can't return to again.

Like memory, at times I wish I could erase
the music of my name in Spanish, at times
I cherish it, and despise my other syllables
clashing in English. *Como tú*, I want to speak

11

of myself in two languages at once. Despite
my tongues, no word defines me. Like words,
I read my footprints like my past, erased by
waves of circumstance, my future uncertain
as wind. Like the wind, *como tú*, I carry songs,
howls, whispers, thunder's growl. Like thunder,
I'm a foreign-borne cloud that's drifted here,
I'm lightning, and the balm of rain. *Como tú*,
our blood rains for the dirty thirst of this land.
Like thirst, like hunger, we ache with the need
to save ourselves, and our country from itself.

STARING AT ASPENS:
A HISTORY LESSON

There were many who died on the way to
Hwééldi. All the way we told each other,
"We will be strong, as long as we are together."
I think that was what kept us alive.

from *In 1864* by LUCI TAPAHONSO

Stare until the trembling leaves are tongues
whispering the Navajo's true name, Diné,
in their language. Listen to the wind breathing
through the branches still alive with the story
of their sacred land cornered by the colors
of their four cardinal mountains. Then look
at the shadowed understory, the dark past
of their homeland: 1864, the scorched earth
policy of the army—their fields raped by fire,
their handmade homes made ash, pottery
smashed, sheep and cattle slaughtered, blood
drawn right before their eyes, and water kept
from their lips. Watch the aspens' boughs break
in a storm and know the anguish of 8,000 Diné
forced to surrender their land, marched away
on the Long Walk, 300 miles to Fort Sumner,
a place they'd call Hwééldi. Each step a sorrow:
the starved sifting horse droppings for seeds
to eat—shot, the elders with buckled knees—
shot, the pregnant women, too slow—shot,
and mothers at gunpoint made to leave babies
cradled in cottonwoods crying to a deaf moon.
Watch the aspen catkins bloom in springtime
and imagine the joy of the Diné four years later

on the Long Walk back, home again to breathe
their air, honor their snow-crowned mountains,
taste their riverwaters, stand amid the stands
of their aspens. Dig into their ground, learn
how aspens are all born from the same roots
they share, how they thrive as many, yet live
as one. Admire the aspen, but praise the Diné
who've survived history as one people, still
one nation. Stare at the aspens until you see
what the Diné never failed to see, stare
until you see all that we've failed to see.

LETTER FROM YÍ CHEUNG
Angel Island Immigration Station, 1938

When I saw you last, rain blessed
the ground orchids, all of Chung Lau
crowded your good face with goodbyes.
You took the long road to Hoi-Ping
to the sea—to America. I was young
as the kapok blooms but did not cry
for you gone. Remember? I cried joy
for the dream you sought for you,
and for me to know someday too.

Twice in age and height now, hair
braided no more, I crossed the seas
you crossed. I am here, so near you,
father, on this island called Angel, but
with no wings to fly me across the bay
between us, with no bridge to your city,
like the glowing bridge I sometimes see
when the fog clears, and I imagine you:
clinging to street cars, tending the soiled
clothes of strangers, thinking of mama
dying without you. But the fog returns
—everything disappears, even hope.

How to say this, father: every day
they take me into a room of cold chairs
and blue eyes. They demand I remember
the streets of my childhood, the names
of our village neighbors, their children,
the colors of their houses. Sometimes

I forget. Sometimes I lie. Sometimes
I answer right, but they do not believe
I am your daughter, even when I speak
your full, honorable name or swear
I know the heart-shape of your face
is like mine. They do not yet let me go.

Months of bitter nights in barracks,
I make myself sleep by counting stars
I no longer see, turning my harsh sighs
into lullabies you once sang like chimes.
I try not to think of the pigeons trapped
and eaten by the men, or the old woman
whose name I knew, when she hanged
herself from her bedsheets in the hall.
I shy from the poems on the walls carved
by some who curse this place, this land,
and its people. I may understand why.

But those words never are mine—
nothing can stop our sun, our moon,
our tides and seasons, nor what I have
dreamed in you, and you in me. Our life
true against hardship, more now as I wish
to be where you are, as you are. But soon
I will have my wings, the fog will forever
clear, your gracious gaze will bless me,
your hand to hold mine, brush my face
like a feather. I will hear your voice call
me to my destiny by the beautiful name
you gave me, meaning: *joy, harmony*.

LEAVING IN THE RAIN:
LIMERICK, IRELAND

for Caroline

I have no exact reason to miss you, your city, nor
this island of yours—like everything, like nothing
I had imagined: the plentiful wisdom of so much
silver rain softening rock, spreading across pillows
of green hills rolling past the train's window leaving
Limerick after only a few days of knowing you, and
my life with your kin, teaching myself by teaching
them to trust a poem's imagery, hear it as music
enough to mend what we ourselves rend apart.

I smiled your smile, answering me: *No, lad, limericks
didn't come from here.* Yet I felt poetry everywhere:
in the brooding walls of King John's Castle against
your grey sky, in the daring of a few rays of sunlight
each day striking the steel and glass of my hotel,
in the granite sparkle of sidewalks solid under foot
on our daily lunchtime strolls to Dunnes for bacon
and pears, also bread to court the seagulls gathered
every afternoon by the River Shannon, its tidal ebb
and flow a recurring dream, you noticed, reminding
me to remember and forget myself twice each day.

Why should your home be home to me? My eyes
belong to another sea, my feet to another island—
Cuba, where rain falls differently. Yet the stranger
on the train across the aisle could be my mother
pulling turquoise yarn from a tote bag on the floor

like a faithful dog sitting beside her swollen ankles.
Her long needles, a soft, rhythmic whetting of steel
against steel, could be a cello in her spotted hands
that don't remember or need her anymore to make
what: socks for her granddaughter, another sweater
for her faraway son, a vest for her dead husband?
Only she knows what she misses, what is, was, or will
be home to her, knows the sorrow in her every stitch
as much as the joy pulled from each loop she purls.

Beside her, a bearded man sleeps, his furrowed brow
and bony hands tell a story like the broken spine
of the book facedown on his lap, parted to words
he couldn't finish—too droll or terrifying for him,
perhaps. I wonder if his eyes are green as ferns
or brown as dirt, if they're dreaming of tigers, or
moonlight echoes, or the timbre of his father's voice.
I wonder if he's leaving home or returning. Maybe
he's a stranger like me, among strangers between
points on the earth to which these tracks are nailed.
Where am I? Where am I going? It doesn't matter.

What matters is the poem in the window: a blurred
watercolor where tree is chimney, chimney is cloud,
cloud is brick, brick is puddle, puddle is rain, and rain
is me, refracted in each luscious bead. How free and
impossible to be everything inside everything I see.
How terribly beautiful never having to say I'm from
here or *there*, never recalling my childhood home
where I played checkers alone, or the royal palms
lining the street where I learned to ride my bike,
or my mango-scented backyard catching fireflies

like stars in glass jars, or my bedroom where I first
heard my voice say, *Richard*, my name breaking
me from the world, the world suddenly broken
into geography, history, weather, language, war.

I would like to die twice, Caroline: once to feel
that last breath flood my body, then come back
to tell of life not pulled apart, not dimensioned—
a seamless mass at light-speed before the dead
stop of the train at 3:05. Before the man wakes up,
closes his book, forgets or vows to live his dream.
Before the woman stuffs her needles into her bag,
stands up, sighs into the ache of her feet. Before
everything becomes itself again: brick into brick,
tree into tree, cloud into cloud, puddle into puddle,
me into me, standing on the platform knowing
Pavese was right: *You need a village, if only for*
the pleasure of leaving it . . . and someday returning
to it, to your city, to you, and the rain we shared.

ISLAND BODY

Forced to leave home, but home
never leaves us. Wherever exile
takes us, we remain this body made
from the red earth of our island—
our ribs taken from its *montes*—
its breeze our breaths. We stand
with its *palmeras*. Our eyes hold
its blue-green sea. Waterfalls
echo in our ears. On our wrists,
jasmine. Our palms open, close
like its hibiscus to love, be loved.

We thrive wherever we remain
true to our *lucha*—the hustle
of our feet walking to work
as we must, our oily hands
fixing all the broken beauty
we must fix, our soiled hands
growing what we must grow,
or cutting what must be cut,
our backs carrying the weight
of our island's sands, our pulse
its waves, our sweat the gossamer
dew and dust of its sunrises,
our voice the song of its *sinsontes*
and its *son* nested in our souls.

Wherever the world spins us,
home remains the island that
remains in us. Its sun still sets

in our eyes, its clouds stay still
above us, our hands still hold
its tepid rain. We're still caught
under its net of stars, still listen to
its moon crooning above its dirt.
roads. We're its rivers, the hem
of its coast and lace of its *sierras*,
its valley windsongs, its vast seas
of green sugarcane fields. We're
our island's sweetness as bitter
as the taste of having to leave it.

WHAT WE DIDN'T
KNOW ABOUT CUBA

for Emilio

Just a hired driver—or so Rita and I thought,
his Cuban-American tourists for the day—
as we drove off from our sea-scoured hotel
in Havana, east to Matanzas, a town known
for great poets, but named after a massacre,
he said, offering us water and mints, looking
at us through the rearview mirror of his dinged
but freshly waxed sedan. The seats faded but
spotless, a cracked windshield but immaculate
dashboard. San Lazaro's sacred but sad eyes
watching from a prayer card tucked in the visor.

A real *macho cubano*, tall in his seat and stiff
as his starched *guayabera*, his eyes hidden
by aviator sunglasses. He spoke only to ask if
we were hungry or needed a restroom, only
gave one-word answers to our questions: Are
you married? [*Sí*] Any children? [*Sí*] Any family
in Miami? [*No*] Would you leave Cuba? [*Sí*].
Much like Rita's father and my own, a man
we'd never quite know—or so it seemed.

We turned our attention, began speaking to
each other in English, believing he only spoke
Spanish. As he kept his eyes on the road, we
kept talking about building cultural bridges to
and from Cuba, wanting to mend it, ourselves.
As he hugged the curves along the coast, we

clung to our ideas about the power of poetry
to create dialog and shape the island's future.
We chatted mile after mile to Matanzas where,
as planned, we spent the day at an art gallery
sharing poems about *our* hopes, *our* losses.

Praised by applause, pleased with ourselves,
we strolled back to the car where he'd waited,
sleeping all afternoon. We had asked him to
join us, but he refused. Minutes after we left
Matanzas, he pulled over near a cliff edging
the azure waters of a cove. *Disculpe*, he said,
and stepped out with his cell phone in hand.
He returned, sighed into his seat, grabbed
San Lazaro and ripped him in half. He tore
his sunglasses off, pinched his eyes—two
hazel stars exploded with sudden tears.

Everything—the seagulls, the palm trees,
their shadows, the sunset, its rusty clouds,
the waves, the wind, and our next breath—
stopped—until he breathed again—yelled
in broken English at the broken windshield:
She gone—left us like nothing! She, his wife,
mother of his son. She, adrift on a raft hoping
for Florida. Her vow of for better or worse . . .
broken like my damn country! Why? he asked,
a rhetorical question, we thought—but no—
it was meant for us: *Why you don't write
a damn poem about this? Why?* he repeated
to us, to the sea, to the horizon, to her ghost
already dawning in dusk's far, fleeting light.

MATTERS OF THE SEA

US Embassy Reopening Ceremony,
Havana, Cuba, August 14, 2015

The sea doesn't matter, what matters is this:
we all belong to the sea between us, all of us
once and still the same child who marvels over
starfish, listens to hollow shells, sculpts dreams
into impossible castles. We've all been lovers,
holding hands, strolling either of our shores—
our footprints like a mirage of selves vanished
in waves that don't know their birth or care
on which country they break. They break, bless
us, return to the sea, home to our silent wishes.

No one is other, to the other, to the sea, whether
on hemmed island or vast continent, remember:
our grandfathers, their hands dug deep into red
or brown earth, planting maple or mango trees
that outlived them; our grandmothers counting
years while dusting photos of their weddings—
brittle family faces still alive on *our* dressers now.
Our mothers teaching us how to read in Spanish
or English, how to tie our shoes, how to gather
fall's colors, or bite into guavas. Our fathers worn
by the weight of clouds, clocking-in at factories,
or cutting sugarcane to earn a new life for us.
My cousins and I now scouting the same stars
above skyscrapers or palms, waiting for time
to stop and begin again when rain falls, washes
its way through river or street, back to the sea.

No matter what anthem we sing, we've all walked
barefoot and bare-souled among the soar and dive
of seagull cries. We've offered our sorrows, hopes
up to the sea, our lips anointed by the same spray
of salt-laden wind. We've fingered our memories
and regrets like stones in our hands we can't toss.
Yet we've all cupped seashells to our ears. Listen
again to the echo—the sea still telling us the end
to our doubts and fears is to gaze into the lucid blues
of our shared horizon, breathe together, heal together.

MOTHER COUNTRY

To love a country as if you've lost one: 1968,
my mother leaves Cuba for America, a scene
I imagine as if standing in her place—one foot
inside a plane destined for a country she knew
only as a name, a color on a map, or glossy photos
from drugstore magazines, her other foot anchored
to the platform of her *patria*, her hand clutched
around one suitcase, taking only what she needs
most: hand-colored photographs of her family,
her wedding veil, the doorknob of her house,
a jar of dirt from her backyard, goodbye letters
she won't open for years. The sorrowful drone
of engines, one last, deep breath of familiar air
she'll take with her, one last glimpse at all
she'd ever known: the palm trees wave goodbye
as she steps onto the plane, the mountains shrink
from her eyes as she lifts off into another life.

To love a country as if you've lost one: I hear her
—*once upon a time*—reading picture books
over my shoulder at bedtime, both of us learning
English, sounding out words as strange as the talking
animals and fair-haired princesses in their pages.
I taste her first attempts at macaroni-n-cheese
(but with chorizo and peppers), and her shame
over Thanksgiving turkeys always dry, but countered
by her perfect pork *pernil* and garlic *yuca*. I smell
the rain of those mornings huddled as one under
one umbrella waiting for the bus to her ten-hour days
at the cash register. At night, the zzz-zzz of her sewing

her own blouses, *quinceañera* dresses for her nieces
still in Cuba, guessing at their sizes, and the gowns
she'd sell to neighbors to save for a rusty white sedan—
no hubcaps, no air-conditioning, sweating all the way
through our first vacation to Florida theme parks.

To love a country as if you've lost one: as if
it were *you* on a plane departing from America
forever, clouds closing like curtains on your country,
the last scene in which you're a madman scribbling
the names of your favorite flowers, trees, and birds
you'd never see again, your address and phone number
you'd never use again, the color of your father's eyes,
your mother's hair, terrified you could forget these.
To love a country as if I was my mother last spring
hobbling, insisting I help her climb all the way up
to the US Capitol, as if she were here before you today
instead of me, explaining her tears, cheeks pink
as the cherry blossoms coloring the air that day when
she stopped, turned to me, and said: You know, *mijo*,
it isn't where you're born that matters, it's where
you choose to die—that's your country.

MY FATHER IN ENGLISH

First half of his life lived in Spanish: the long syntax
of *las montañas* that lined his village, the rhyme
of *sol* with his soul—a Cuban *alma*—that swayed
with *las palmas*, the sharp rhythm of his *machete*
cutting through *caña*, the syllables of his *canarios*
that sung into *la brisa* of the island home he left
to spell out the second half of his life in English—
the vernacular of New York City sleet, neon, glass—
and the brick factory where he learned to polish
steel twelve hours a day. Enough to save enough
to buy a used Spanish-English dictionary he kept
bedside like a bible—studied fifteen new words
after his prayers each night, then practiced them
on us the next day: *Buenos días, indeed, my family.*
Indeed más coffee. Have a good day today, indeed—
and again in the evening: *Gracias to my bella wife,*
indeed, for dinner. Hicistes tu homework, indeed?
La vida is indeed difícil. Indeed did indeed become
his favorite word which, like the rest of his new life,
he never quite grasped: overused and misused often
to my embarrassment. Yet the word I most learned
to love and know him through: *indeed*, the exile who
tried to master the language he chose to master him,
indeed, the husband who refused to say *I love you*
in English to my mother, the man who died without
true translation. *Indeed*, meaning: in fact/*en efecto*,
meaning: in reality/*de hecho*, meaning to say now
what I always meant to tell him in both languages:
thank you/*gracias* for surrendering the past tense
of your life so that I might conjugate myself here
in the present of this country, in truth/*así es, indeed.*

EL AMERICANO IN THE MIRROR

Maybe you don't remember, or don't want to, or
maybe, like me, you've never been able to forget:
May 1979, fifth-grade recess, I grabbed your collar,
shoved you up against the wall behind the chapel,
called you a sissy-ass *americano* to your face, then
punched you—hard as I could. Maybe you still live,
as I do, with the awful crack of my knuckles' slam
on your jaw, and the grim memory of your lip split.

Why didn't you punch me back? That would've hurt
less than the jab of your blue eyes dulled with pain—
how you let your body wilt, lean into me, and we
walked arm in arm to the boys' room, washed off
the blood and dirt. Is that how you remember it?
What you can't remember is what I thought when
our gazes locked in the mirror and I wanted to say:
I'm sorry, maybe *I love you*. Perhaps even kiss you.

Did you feel it, too? At that instant did we both
somehow understand what I'm only now capable
of putting into these words: that I didn't hate you,
but envied you—the *americano* sissy I wanted to be
with sheer skin, dainty freckles, the bold consonants
of your English name, your perfectly starched shirts,
pleated pants, that showy *Happy Days* lunchbox,
your A-plus spelling quizzes that I barely passed.

Why didn't you snitch on me? I don't remember now
who told Sister Magdalene, but I'll never forget how
she wrung my ears until I cried for you, dragged me

to the back of the room, made me stand for the rest
of that day, praying the rosary to think hard about
my sins. And I did, I have for thirty-two years, Derek.
Whether you don't remember, don't want to, or never
forgot: forgive me, though I may never forgive myself.

USING COUNTRY IN A SENTENCE

My chair is *country* to my desk. The empty page
    is *country* to my lifelong question of *country*
turning like a grain of sand irritating my mind, still
    hoping for some pearly answer. My question
is *country* to my imagination, reimagining *country*,
    not as our stoic eagle, but as wind, the *country*
its feathers and bones must muster to soar, eye
    its kill of mice. The wind's *country* as the clouds
it chisels into hieroglyphs to write its voice across
    blank skies. A mountain as *country* to the clouds
that crown and hail its peak, then drift, betray it
    for some other majesty. No matter how tall
mountains may rise, they're bound to the *country*
    that raises them and grinds them back into
earth, a borderless *country* to its rooted armies
    of trees standing as sentinel, their branches
country to every leaf, each one a tiny *country*
    to every drop of rain it holds like a breath
for a moment, then must let go. Rain's *country*,
    the sea from which it's exiled into the sky
as vapor. The sky an infinite, universal *country*,
    its citizens the tumultuous stars turning
like a kaleidoscope above my rooftop and me
    tonight. My glass as *country* to the wine I sip,
my lips *country* to my thoughts on the half moon
    —a *country* of light against shadow, like ink
against paper, my hand as *country* to my fingers,
    to my words asking if my home is the only
country I need to have, or if my *country* is the only
    home I have to need. And I write: *country*—
end it with a question mark. Lay my pen to rest.

II

AMERICAN WANDERSONG

I celebrate myself, and sing myself,
And what I assume you shall assume,
For every atom belonging to me
   as good belongs to you.

WALT WHITMAN
Song of Myself

Yo vengo de todas partes,
Y hacia todas partes voy:
Arte soy entre las artes,
En los montes, monte soy.

JOSÉ MARTÍ
Versos Sencillos

For my parents' exile from their blood-warm rain of Cuba to Madrid's frozen drizzle pinging rooftops the February afternoon I was born. A tiny brown and wrinkled blessing counter to such poverty that my first crib was an open drawer cushioned with towels in an apartment shared by four families. Such as my mother told me for years, kindling my imagination still burning to understand that slipping into being when my longing to belong first began.

And continued: swaddled in the cloud of her arms above the clouds of the Atlantic to America, birthed again at forty-five days old as an immigrant, my newborn photo taken for my green card. Destined to live with two first languages, two countries, two selves, and in the space between them all.

My name is and isn't *Ricardo De Jesús Blanco-Valdés*—christened for the sunlit and sea-song past of my parents' island, carrying withered memories of their homeland like dry rose petals pressed in a book that someday I'd need to crack open, read into the middle of a story I'd need to reclaim, finish, and call my own.

My name is and isn't Richard, a translation I began to call myself by, yearning to write myself into my other story, my other role, my other fictional character as a straight white boy of color in an American drama I didn't quite understand, either.

· · ·

For the terra-cotta roof and tattered lawn chair patio of the home that raised me in Miami, soothed by the mango tree shadows of our backyard. Their tangy-ripe scent stirring in with the incense of *comino* and *laurel* rising from *Mamá's* pots of *frijoles negros*, the taste of my birthright at dinner every night.

My father listening to 8-tracks of Cuban *danzones*, slumped in the family room sofa alone with a glass full of rum and empty eyes. My *Abuelo's* front-porch stories of all *we* lost to *la revolución*: *our* farmhouse, *our* jasmine trees, *our* dog, Pancho. My *Abuela* steadying me down the driveway, insisting I learn how to ride my bike and be *el hombre* she knew I'd never be.

The papery curtains of my bedroom fluttering with the speech-less moon that spoke to me about loneliness, distance, journey, echoed by the palm tree sways against my window rustling a lullaby every night while I mumbled my prayers in English, then Spanish: glory be to all the light and the shadow, the wonder and noise, the confusion and calm of my childhood—*as it was in the beginning, is now, and ever shall be, world without end. Amen.*

. . .

For the end of that sinless child when I began to question why god was love—everywhere and in everything—yet I belonged nowhere and to no one, unable to love even myself or let myself be loved. Even after I dared love men instead of women, and my youth burst like the dusk-red blooms of the poincianas, their beauty surrendered all at once. I withered like their petals strewn over the same city streets I wore down driving to night-clubs where I needed to feel at home under dancefloor lights and against the stubble of men with phone numbers I knew not to call, inked on cocktail napkins or my forearm.

Those lovesick nights that dead-ended with a sunrise on the beach, wading through my ache in every wave dying at my feet. My

36

mind hovering with the seagulls screeching questions into the wind, terrified I'd never belong to anything but anonymous sky. The skyline's trove of ruby and diamond lights waning over the bay like sinking treasure, my city the fortune I knew someday I'd have to abandon and lose to memory.

. . .

For the day I had to drive away: nine hundred miles for seventeen hours straight to New Orleans in my convertible: top down, wind tousling my hair and mind, my ears breathing in the melancholy notes of any sad song I could find on the radio: *Fire and Rain, Landslide, Dust in the Wind.* Singing along into the windshield, my eyes catching themselves in the rearview mirror, then looking away to keep speeding away from the self I was in Miami toward another self I wanted to bump into striding down Royal Street. Treat him to a swig of bourbon at a jazzy lounge, tell his eyes: *I love you, man, you belong here with me.*

I couldn't find that *me*, until it started raining. There's nothing like rain in New Orleans to forget yourself. It shatters everything. It shattered me like glass, gritty, glittery as the woman's voice that seduced me into La Bon Vie. A hibiscus tucked in her hair and a spotlight on her soul as she finished her set crooning: *good morning, heartache, sit down.* I sat next to her at the end of the bar. Asked her name. She wouldn't say. But I bought her a whiskey anyway for the loss I saw fathomed in her eyes, as brown and dazed as mine. We cheered to lives like the city split by the Mississippi, its waters murky yet always flowing, an incessant filling and emptying of itself, like myself.

. . .

For New York's skyscrapers gleaming like proud kings in a giant game of chess I wanted to master and win. Though I was only a pawn that weekend, riding the click-clack of subways in sync with my heartbeat. Uptown to El Barrio to taste the Spanish of my Puerto Rican kin, their street vendors' icy *piraguas* and steamy *pasteles*. Downtown to stare into the gap left by the towers and my regret for the 9/11 poem I never wrote because I didn't love or hate America enough, then. Then Midtown to gaze at Van Gogh and Matisse, trying to reconcile the truth of art owned by a city whose art is also true greed.

And yet, always the light atop the stairwell beckoning me up toward its grand avenues to imagine a new life as vivid and rude as the yellow streaks of its taxi cabs, as necessary and imposing as its bridges, as sweet-n-sour as the exhaust swirling through its avenues, as charged as its brigade of shoulders hurtling down gum-blotched sidewalks crowded with opportunities fresh as its fruit stands, powerful yet dismal as its jumbotron nights swallowing every star whole. Could I live a life without stars?

. . .

For the blackbirds perched like commas on the telephone wire strung outside my kitchen window like a sentence scrawled in a language as foreign to me as Hartford's granite mansions and grist mills, its white-washed steeples and snuffed-out smokestacks. All like another country to me, feeling my parents' exile as my own, thinking I deserved it for believing that to be an American meant betraying the mango and palm trees that raised me for the winter skeletons of the birches, as beautiful as they were lonely, as I was among them, barely surviving along the grey stretch of Grandview Avenue on my drive to the university to teach how poems sing and save.

Yet what saved me then was my neighbor who fed me cannoli, espresso, and the strums of her guitar recasting steel skies into the cobalt notes of Segovia. What salvaged me was the man who found my eyes over a martini, held my hand down the trail at Talcott Mountain along the reservoir, listened with me to the ice sheets groaning and shifting like my life. The man I married for teaching me how to read William James, how to sauté shallots with filet mignon, how to make my first snow angel amid the frozen souls of the rose garden at Elizabeth Park.

. . .

For all the photos I've taken wandering, wanting to capture myself in-love with a country I could not simply live with, but could also die with. See me here: pocketing a stone from the Colosseum as a souvenir of how an empire or a life crumbles under the weight of its own excess. See me: out of breath atop Fuego volcano wanting to mix my blood with the earth's blood in its crater, simmering with Guatemala's revolutions. See me: inside the dungeon walls of the Palazzo Ducale carved with the last words of the condemned. Hear me: imagining, dreading the last poem I would ever carve.

Here I was: sinking with the mortal wealth of Venice's chandeliers and marble floors. Here I was: showered by a Brazilian waterfall in el Rio das Almas, River of Souls, flowing through the hillside resorts of Pirenópolis and the village women beating their wash against its rocks. Here I was: on the top floor of La Grande Arche de la Défense, overlooking the luminous anatomy of Paris, so beautiful it hurt like a lover I can never possess and must abandon. Here I was, wherever I was: lost in always trying to find someplace, someone, something to belong to, yet always returning to myself. Here I am, again.

. . .

For the half of me who never lived in Cuba, yet remembers it as if I was returning to its chartreuse fields and turquoise-laced coasts coloring my eyes again for the first time as the plane descends toward the land of which I am a descendant. I step into a mirage of myself haunted by impossible memories of who I was and would be had my life been lived here.

The boy who hacks into the flesh of coconuts I never tasted, who reads time from the village clock in the square where I never played marbles with my cousins, who pedals through country roads raising dust that never raised me, who catches fireflies that I never chased, the neon green flashes that never dazzled my childhood here.

The son who slashes sugarcane I never harvested with my father, adores him as I never did for his careworn hands that never held mine, my hands around his waist riding his horse that I never rode to the dirt-floor home where I never grew up watching my mother stir pots of *arroz-con-pollo* in a kitchen where I never ate, and never listened to bedtime stories she never told me in a bed where I never dreamed.

The man who misses a life I never knew was mine to miss, claim as my own in Spanish, as *muy mío*: the conga beats of my tropical storms, ballad of my *palmeras*, balmy whispers of my Caribbean song. *Muy mío*: the iron-red soil of my flesh, sand of my white bones, pink hibiscus of my blood. *Muy mío*: the constellations I reconfigure into an astrology to read the past of who this half of me was, or never was. The future of who I will never be, or who will always be as an island within this island, *muy mío*.

. . .

For the destiny of desire that drove the Potomac's course and mine here, to live along its marshy banks in a colonial townhouse with flower boxes and shelves of poetry I hauled to teach my students questions the other half of me had been asking all my life: What of my love for this country, my faith in its ideals? I heard faint answers through its capital's streets: *We the people* waiting at traffic lights and metro stops. *Justice for all* echoed in statues' eyes and every fountain's trickle. *A more perfect union* breezing through its marble colonnades and beaming off its glorious domes.

Like a tourist wanting to be a native, I said *yes* to all of it. Yes, to the glow of the full moon I caught aglow with promises teetering at the tip of the Washington Monument. Yes, to a fistful of cherry blossoms I praised as delicate as our democracy. Yes, to the veins of my hands pressed against the granite veins of the Vietnam Memorial, standing beside a veteran with only one arm and one rose for one name he thanked for saving his life. Yes, to hating myself for acknowledging the innateness of war, empire, and also the privilege it granted me.

But also—yes—to my duty to contest it, try to shape its story with my deeds and words, with the inaugural poem I'd write ten years later and read before the National Mall looking out into the mirror of a million faces like mine, like so many of us, still hoping to belong and heal as one, under one sun, over one nation. Yes to the half of me I recognized in the reflecting pool capturing the Lincoln Memorial and the wisdom chiseled in his eyes, still speaking to us today: yes, *a house divided cannot stand.* Nor can I.

. . .

For the whole of me steeped in this dusk before the stars embroider the sky and the Milky Way's swatch appears above the back porch of my life in Maine. Needing to be nowhere and no one but this stillness: a drop of rain on my eave just before it swells and adjourns into the ground, a hummingbird paused at my buttercup, my honeysuckle vine before it inches another inch, my still pond just before the ripple from a frog's leap or a loose stone's fall, the content maple leaves before the October wind stirs and chills my hillside and my bones.

For now: the fixed geometry of the White Mountains that needn't move or heed a thing, drawn across my window, for now: a spider patient at the center of its web spun across my doorway, for now: my peonies satisfied with the beautiful weight of their immense blooms, for now: my ferns like flags that unfurl, wither, and unfurl again, loyal to the same ground. For now: my wandersong the carol of robins perched in my pear tree, my soul the wisps of these clouds tendering the watercolor sunset. For now: I am citizen of these dimming skies, in the country of my body, homeland to myself—for just a moment.

III

IMAGINARY EXILE

Dawn breaks my window and dares me
to write a poem brave enough to imagine
the last day I'll ever see this amber light
color the wind breathing life into the dark
faces of these mountains I know by name,
risen from the bedrock of the only country
I've truly lived, resting on the same earth
as this house in which I'll never rise again—

a poem that captures me making my bed
one last time as the sun climbs the maples
I'll never again watch burst like fireworks
into fall, or undress themselves, slip into
snow's white lace. Never again the spring
giggles of my brook, or creaks of my floor.
Never the scent of my peonies or pillows.
Never my eyes on my clouds, or my ears
to the rain on my rooftop in this country—

a poem that finds a word for the emptiness
of suddenly becoming a stranger in my own
kitchen, as I sip my last cup of coffee, linger
with the aroma of my last meal, my hands
trembling as I toss leftovers, wash dishes,
eat one last piece of bread I'll never break
again, and cork a half-empty bottle of wine
I'll never finish, a vintage I'll keep savoring
like memories through my mind's palate—

a poem that lists which parts of me to part
with, or take: Give up my orchids and dog
to my neighbor Jewel, but keep our stares
goodbye. Leave the china and crystal, but
box the plastic souvenirs. Forget my books,
but pack every letter and card I've saved.
Not the gold chains that won't buy back
my life, but stuff all the loose photos like
crumbs in my pockets I'll need to survive—

a poem that brings daisies for my mother,
holds her as I swear I'll return to hold her
again, though we both know I never will.
That speaks with my father one last time
at his grave, and forgives his silence again,
forever. That hopes my husband can flee
with me, knowing he can't—our last gaze
a kiss meaning more to us than our first,
as I hold his hand and hand him my keys—

a poem ending as I walk backwards away
from his love at my door to open another—
step into some strange house and country
to harden into a statue of myself, my eyes
fixed and crumbling like the moon, and like
the moon, live by borrowed light, always but
never quite, dying in the sky, never forgiving
my fate, in a poem I never want to write.

NOVEMBER EYES

I question everyone, everything, even the sun
as I drive east down Main Street—radio off—
to Amy's diner. She bobby-pins her hair, smiles
her usual *good mornin'* but her eyes askew say
something like: *You believe this?* as she wipes
the counter, tosses aside the *Journal Times*—
the election headlines as bitter as the coffee
she pours for me without a blink. After a cup
and a blueberry muffin I remember my bills
are due by the fifteenth—so I cross on Main
to the post office. Those American Flag stamps
are all Debbie has left. I refuse to buy them:
a *never mind* in my eyes which she dismisses
with a gesture of *suit yourself.* Bills can wait,
but not my dog's treats or the milk I'm out of
—so I drive up Main again to the Food Basket.
Paper or plastic, Jan asks me at the checkout,
but it doesn't matter. What matters is this:
she's been to my bar-b-ques, I've donated
to her son's football league, we've shoveled
each other's driveways, we send each other
Christmas cards. She knows I'm Latino and
gay. Yet suddenly I don't know who she is
as I read the button on her polyester vest:
Trump: Make America Great Again, meaning
she doesn't *really* know me either. We manage
smiles when she hands me my change, but
our locked eyes say: nothing—so I dash off—
go see Tom at the bank to cash a measly check
from some *grand* magazine for some *grand*
poem of mine loaded with some *grand* words

like *transcend*, as if my inked verbs could bend
a river's will, shuffle stars, change the fate of
our nation, or the blur in Tom's eyes thinking
what I think of our reflection on the bullet-
proof window, asking: *So now what, Mr. Poet?*
I can't answer. I can only remember today
I'm supposed to buy a rake, lightbulbs, nails
to hang my aging mother's photos—so I swing
by Union Hardware, see Dan who knows me,
and what I need. He rings me up, doesn't say
Goodbye, says *Good luck*, as if his eyes can see
the uncertainty in my own, worried about:
my immigrant cousin, factory jobs, groped
women, hijabs, blacklists, bans, the church,
the deep state, cops, race, and which lives
matter, hacked votes, refugee camps, dead
children, missiles, suicide bombers, carbon
footprints, polar bears, sunk islands, my gay
marriage, the bills for my preexisting ulcer
flaring, guns at malls, guns at schools, guns
at clubs, more guns, more corporate rights,
soulless cubicles, the empty Supreme Court
seats, the border wall, bullying, the demise
of language, news, the silence of suspicion,
the uneasy guessing, the surprise of who's
who, the cheers and gloating, or jeers and
swearing, the final picking of sides, right or
left, red or blue state, city, or town, but no
grey today except for the November clouds
looming over Main Street with all the rest
of our unrest, arrested in our eyes clashing
against each other's glares, ready for battle.

LET'S REMAKE AMERICA GREAT

Yes: Let's re-shoot America as a fantasy, a '50s TV show in clear
   black and white, sponsored by Kent cigarettes, Wonder Bread,
   and good old-fashioned war, again. Let's re-create the backlot
   suburb with rows of five bedroom homes for every Wilson
   and Johnson, walled by perfectly trimmed hedges, weedless
   lawns, and at least one 12-cylinder sedan parked in every drive-
   way, in the right neighborhood, again.

Let's recast every woman as a housewife, white and polite as Don-
   na Reed always glowing on the kitchen set, again. Let's direct
   them to adore making and serving deviled eggs, tuna casse-
   role, apple pies from scratch, again, costumed in pleated skirts
   and pearl chokers, aprons as immaculate as their thoughts—no
   lines about a career or rape, again. Let's re-create *Bewitched*, but
   keep the same script for all women to follow, again: Samantha
   —blonde and busty, of course—but a real witch who tames
   her powers for the love of fetching her husband's slippers and
   stirring his martinis, again.

Let's write-out women like my mother, who fled Cuba broken as
   her broken English, who cooked dinner in her uniform after
   twelve-hour shifts at the supermarket, set the table with plastic
   cups she could rinse out and reuse. Let's cast her as a maid,
   though even the help needs to be white and proud, again. No
   roles for Mexican nannies and gardeners unless they are mur-
   derers, nor black businessmen unless they are armed drug deal-
   ers, nor Muslim taxi drivers unless they are terrorists, again.

Let's give every leading role to men like Jim from *Father Knows Best*,
   never dangerous, never weak, never poor, always white with a
   great job and time to page their newspapers, lounge in their
   wing chairs in command of their wives, their children, and the

49

plot, again. Let's not consider true-to-life parts for men like my immigrant father, who had to work as a butcher all day, help my mother wash the dishes, then clean offices all night. Always too tired to say: *I love you champ*, and kiss me goodnight. Never enough time to be the father, man he wanted to be, again.

Let's audition only straight boys like Opie, who carry slingshots and fishing poles, catch crickets and frogs, who don't play patty-cakes with girls or grow up to marry a man like I did. Let's keep gay characters in the closet for the camera, again: keep Miss Hathaway in skirt suits with cropped hair and single at forty, but keep her mad crush on Jethro, again; keep Uncle Arthur in his floral-print ascots with his hand on his hip, dishing out campy gossip, but keep him acting like a true lady's man, again.

Let's remake America as great as it never really was: Take two. Quiet on the set.

EASY LYNCHING ON
HERNDON AVENUE

What I'd rather not see isn't here: no rope,
no black body under a white moon swaying
limp from a tree, no bloodied drops of dew
on the twenty-first of March 1981. That's
in another photo, like a dozen other photos
I've gaped at wanting—not wanting—to turn
away from the snapped necks of the hanged,
and the mob's smug smirks, asking myself
How could they? Why? Questions not here,
not in this photo—a crisp and tranquil snap-
shot—murder washed out by time, history
left uncaptured. What's left now is easier
on our eyes: only pale morning light seeping
blue into the sky—a backdrop to the necks
of tree boughs bowing like swans, innocent
of any crime on Herndon Avenue, pictured like
any other street: clean sidewalks (no blood),
utility poles strung with wires (no rope), a few
pavement cracks (no broken-boned body).

Easier to imagine only this: groomed children
waiting for the school bus grinding to a halt
that March morning, the twenty-first, 1981.
Their backpacks zipped with undoubtable
history and equations, cartoon lunchboxes
filled with fresh ham sandwiches and sweet
grapes. Sport-coat fathers dashing to work,
worried about paychecks and the greenness
of their lawns. All-day mothers left tending

silk pillows never fluffed enough, scrubbing
sinks never white enough, wiping windows
never spotless enough. Easier not to ask if
anyone saw him, if anyone knew the boy
whose mama had named Michael—Michael
Donald. Easier to think no one was friendly
with Mr. Hays and Mr. "Tiger" Knowles who,
on the night of March twenty-first 1981,
drove around looking for something black
to kill at random. They spotted him, age 19,
walking home (the body), strangled him first,
then slit his throat (the blood), chose a tree
to hang him (the rope) on Herndon Avenue.

Why? Which tree was it that shook with
his last breath? Easier not to look for it, not
find it, not make ourselves imagine Michael
still hanging on Herndon Avenue, his death
still alive since March twenty-first, 1981.
Easier not to look at his shut eyes, wonder
what his favorite color or superhero was, if
he liked to skateboard or draw, if he heard
his mama's cries: *My boy—Jesus, my boy!*
Easier to believe the last words on the lips
of his murderers must've been: *Forgive us,*
to trust this kind of thing doesn't happen
anymore, stay blind (no rope, no blood,
no body) to the life of a boy named Michael
invisible in this photo, that is, until we dare
to look hard and deep and long enough.

POETRY ASSIGNMENT #4:
WHAT DO YOU MISS MOST?

Germaine, your poem this week is quite striking—so heartfelt and full of captivating imagery, right from the start.

> *I miss the sun replaced by fluorescent lights*
> *flickering in my cell. I miss the sky, a kinder*
> *blue than the sapphire police lights still*
> *spinning in my memory. I miss the moon,*
> *a gentler shine than the guards' badges*
> *as steely as their blue eyes piercing me.*

You continue with even more powerful images that describe your isolation.

> *I'm smoke trapped in a jar, a star behind*
> *a wall of clouds. I'm a garden of shadows.*

Impressive. Your love for poetry during your college days really shows through. But I'm especially taken by the lines that confess your true "want."

> *More than the sun, the sky, or the moon,*
> *I want my son. I've become nothing but*
> *want, but my want and I are locked up.*

A powerful turn where you truly open up to the emotional core of the poem and begin speaking to your son directly.

> *Son: see my hand still tying the red shoelaces*
> *on your silver Nikes. Taste the Rocky Road*
> *ice cream dripping from our chins. Watch*
> *us watching Batman on our lumpy couch.*
> *Remember when I was your hero? Hear*

us still singing our favorite hip-hop songs—
lyrics of lives we knew by heart. Remember
the plastic handcuffs you played with, not
the metal handcuffs that took me away.

Those vivid and tenderly rendered details really bring your son to life. They let me miss and mourn him as you do when you reveal that he died while you were jailed. You close the poem perfectly by grounding it in imagery that lets us feel your sorrow and emptiness.

Words are my only escape now. In this poem,
I turn iron bars into shadows I walk through
to see your eyes shine, hold your lifeless face
in my palms, kiss your cold forehead goodbye.
In this poem, I curse God and myself—wail
my amens, join the sobbing choir at church.
In this poem I turn back time, stop the bullet,
draw blood back into your body. In this poem,
I save you and you save me from myself.

ST. LOUIS: PRAYER BEFORE DAWN

Watch the dark sky mute amid the vigil of stars, a black-and-white prayer:

Where there is hatred, let me sow love. Amen.

Hear it above Delmar Boulevard with its black-and-white stripes that divide the city into black-and-white voices.

A time to rend, and a time to sew.

Listen to its northside: the din of gunfire, the silence of boarded-up windows, the vagabond weeds creeping through the floorboards of abandoned homes still echoing with children who prayed every night:

And if I die before I wake . . . Amen.

Now listen to its southside: chit-chat about vacation spots, stock tips, and the alabaster blooms of dogwoods in gardens tended to by the help.

The meek shall inherit the earth.

Look into their shimmering windows framing cocktail parties filled with platters of gourmet cheese, fresh-cut flowers, and the bouquet of merlot.

The Lord is my shepherd; I shall not want. Amen.

Don't close your eyes to the sooty plumes of smokestacks rising like sinister incense tarnishing the moon.

Where there is despair, hope.

Compare it to the silver moonlight showering suburban rooftops, backyard decks, green lawns, and the Luna moths' green angel wings.

For it is in giving that we receive. Amen.

Churn with the Mississippi's waters as brown as the skin of the homeless with names, but no home except their shadows in an alley off Market Street.

Blessed are the poor in spirit: theirs is the kingdom of
Heaven. Amen.

Rest with them trying to rest under the arresting reign of fluorescent lights falling twenty stories from locked-up office buildings, empty of executives, but stocked with wealth.

Easier for a camel to go through the eye of a needle than
for a rich man to enter the kingdom of God.

Sleep past dawn with faces resting on tender pillows, asleep under thick comforters.

Grant that I may not so much seek to be consoled as to
console. Amen.

Wake up with faces on buses riding past the graffitied walls of their streets mirroring the truth of their lives on their way to tend boutique hotel rooms, wash shirts and press skirts, or cast concrete floors for luxury condos.

Where there is doubt, faith.

See the arch: not shimmering steel, but dull as nickel in the dark, a broken circle, a broken promise. Not a gateway, but a gate closed on St. Louis, trapped in all its black-and-white.

Yea, though I walk through the valley of the shadow of death,
I will fear no evil. Amen.

Glory be waiting for the dawn. Glory be knowing the only dream worth dreaming is the one we dream in every color.

Where there is darkness, light. Amen.

UNTIL WE COULD

for Mark

I knew it then—when we first found our eyes,
in our eyes, and everything around us—even
the din and smoke of the city—disappeared,
leaving us alone as if we were the only two
men in the world, two mirrors face-to-face:
my reflection in yours, yours in mine, infinite.

I knew since I knew you—but we couldn't.

I caught the sunlight pining through the shears,
traveling millions of dark miles simply to graze
your skin as I did that first dawn I studied you
sleeping beside me: I counted your eyelashes,
read your dreams like butterflies flitting under
your eyelids and ready to flutter into the room.
Yes, I praised you like a majestic creature god
forgot to create, till that morning of you tamed
in my arms, first for me to see, name you mine.
Yes, to the rise and fall of your body, your every
exhale and inhale a breath I breathed as my own
wanting to keep even the air between us as one.

Yes to all of you. Yes I knew, but still we couldn't.

I taught you how to dance *Salsa* by looking
into my Caribbean eyes. You learned to speak
in my tongue, while teaching me how to catch
a snowflake in my palms, love the grey clouds
of your worn-out hometown. Our years began

collecting in glossy photos time-lining our lives
across shelves and walls glancing back at us:
Us embracing in *some* sunset, more captivated
by each other than the sky brushed plum-rose.
Us claiming *some* mountain that didn't matter
as much our climbing it, together. Us leaning
against columns of ruins as ancient as our love
was new, or leaning into our dreams at a table
flickering candlelight in our full-mooned eyes.

I knew *me* as much as *us*, and yet we couldn't.

Though I forgave your blue eyes turning green
each time you lied, kept believing you, though
we managed to say good morning after muted
nights in the same bed, though every door slam
told me to hold on by letting us go, and saying
you're right became as true as saying *I'm right*,
till there was nothing a long walk couldn't solve:
holding hands and hope under the streetlights
lustering like a string of pearls guiding us home,
or a stroll along the beach with our dog, the sea
washed out by our smiles, our laughter roaring
louder than the waves. Though we understood
our love was the same as our parents, though
we dared to tell them so, and they understood.

Though we knew, we couldn't—no one could.

When fiery kick lines and fires were set for us
by our founding mother-fathers at Stonewall,
we first spoke of *defiance*. When we paraded

glitter, leather, and rainbows, our word then
became *pride* down city streets, demanding:
Just let us be. But that wasn't enough. Parades
became rallies—bold words on signs, shouting
until we all claimed freedom as another word
for marriage and said: *Let us in*, insisted: *love
is love*, proclaimed it into all eyes that would
listen at any door that would open, until *noes*
and *maybes* turned into *yeses*, town by town,
city by city, state by state, understanding us
and all those who dared to say *enough* until
the gavel struck into law what we always knew:

Love is the right to say: *I do* and *I do* and *I do* . . .

and I do want us to see every tulip we've planted
come up spring after spring, a hundred more years
of dinners cooked over a shared glass of wine, and
a thousand more movies in bed. I do until our eyes
become voices speaking without speaking, until
like a cloud meshed into a cloud, there's no more
you, me—our names useless. I do want you to be
the last face I see—your breath my last breath,

I do, I do and will and will for those who still can't

vow it yet, but know love's exact reason as much
as they know how a sail keeps the wind without
breaking, or how roots dig a way into the earth,
or how the stars open their eyes to the night, or
how a vine becomes one with the wall it loves, or
how, when I hold you, you are rain in my hands.

BETWEEN [ANOTHER DOOR]

[the door] Between playing dress-up, parading in his mother's pleated skirt, marvelous as her clip-on ruby earrings, or noosed in his father's necktie, cuffed by his wristwatch ticking with his pulse. [the door] Between playing house with his cousin's Barbie dolls, or careening his toy truck through backyard mud. [the door] Between the coloring book prince he was supposed to be, and made to color in blue, or the princess dress he dreamed of wearing, colored in pink. [the door] Between the Wonder Woman lunchbox he pleaded for at KMart, or the Superman backpack his grandmother chose for him. [the door] Between his face slapped for putting on a plastic tiara at Craft World, or praised by his grandfather for wielding his plastic sword. [the door] Between cowboys shooting Indians with his brother's cap gun, or sipping make-believe tea with his cat Ferby. [the door] Between what he could grow up to be: a doctor or nurse; a fireman or secretary; an astronaut or housewife; but never both. [the door] Between hula-hooping with the girls at recess, or dodging the boys who'd trip him, shove him, bruise him. [the door] Between the razzle-dazzle of pom-poms he longed to shake, or the boredom of football games he couldn't follow. [the door] Between the soft wrist of the first girl he held hands with, or the stubble of the first man he kissed. [the door] Between mother's head-bowed shame at the dinner table and his fear of father's inch-wide belt on the hook. [the door] Between their small-talk about his homework, and their silences about his *friends*. [the door] Between lying to a priest upright in his chair, or lying with his truth on a therapist's couch. [the door] Between playing it straight, or leaving town for the rest of his life. [the door] Between loving the only way he could love, or loving a gun to his head, or opening [another door].

ONE PULSE—ONE POEM

Here, sit at my kitchen table, we need to write this
together. Take a sip of *café con leche*, breathe in
the steam and our courage to face this page, bare
as our pain. Curl your fingers around mine, curled
around my pen, hold it like a talisman in our hands
shaking, eyes swollen. But let's not start with tears,
or the flashing lights, the sirens, nor the faint voice
over the cell phone when you heard "I love you . . ."
for the very last time. No, let's ease our way into this,
let our first lines praise the plenitude of morning,
the sun exhaling light into the clouds. Let's imagine
songbirds flocked at my window, hear them chirping
a blessing in Spanish: *bendición-bendición-bendición*

Begin the next stanza with a constant wind trembling
every palm tree, yet steadying our minds just enough
to write out: *bullets, bodies, death*—the vocabulary
of violence raging in our minds, but still mute, choked
in our throats. Leave some white space for a moment
of silence, then fill it with lines repeating the rhythms
pulsing through Pulse that night—salsa, deep house,
electro, merengue, and techno heartbeats mixed with
gunshots. Stop the echoes of that merciless music
with a tender simile to honor the blood of our blood,
without writing *blood*. Use warm words to describe
the cold bodies of our husbands, lovers, and wives,
our sisters, brothers, and friends. Draw a metaphor
so we can picture the choir of their invisible spirits
rising with the smoke toward disco lights, imagine
ourselves dancing with them until the very end.

. . .

Write one more stanza—now. Set the page ablaze
with the anger in the hollow ache of our bones—
anger for the new hate, same as the old kind of hate
for the wrong skin color, for the accent in a voice,
for the love of those we're not supposed to love.
Anger for the voice of politics armed with lies, fear
that holds democracy at gunpoint. But let's not
end here. Turn the poem, find details for the love
of the lives lost, still alive in photos—spread them
on the table, give us their wish-filled eyes glowing
over birthday candles, their unfinished sandcastles,
their training-wheels, Mickey Mouse ears, tiaras.
Show their blemished yearbook faces, silver-teeth
smiles and stiff prom poses, their tasseled caps
and gowns, their first true loves. And then share
their very last selfies. Let's place each memory
like a star, the light of their past reaching us now,
and always, reminding us to keep writing until
we never need to write a poem like this again.

SEVENTEEN FUNERALS

Seventeen suns rising in seventeen bedroom windows. Thirty-four eyes blooming open with the light of one more morning. Seventeen reflections in the bathroom mirror. Seventeen backpacks or briefcases stuffed with textbooks or lesson plans. Seventeen *good mornings* at kitchen breakfasts and seventeen *goodbyes* at front doors. Seventeen drives through palm-lined streets and miles of crammed highways to Marjory Stoneman Douglas High School at 5901 Pine Island Road. The first bell ringing in one last school day on February fourteenth, 2018. Seventeen echoes of footsteps down hallways for five class periods: algebra, poetry, biology, art, history. Seventeen hands writing on whiteboards or taking notes at their desks until the first gunshot at 2:21pm. One AR-15 rifle in the hands of a nineteen year old mind turning hate for himself into hate for others, into one hundred fifty bullets fired in six minutes through building number twelve. Seventeen dead carried down hallways they walked, past cases of trophies they won, flyers for clubs they belonged to, lockers they won't open again. Seventeen Valentine's Day dates broken and cards unopened. Seventeen bodies to identify, dozens of photo albums to page through and remember their lives. Seventeen caskets and burial garments to choose for them. Seventeen funerals to attend in twelve days. Seventeen graves dug and headstones placed—all marked with the same date of death. Seventeen names: Alyssa. Helena. Scott. Martin—seventeen absentees forever—Nicholas. Aaron. Jamie. Luke—seventeen closets to clear out—Christopher. Cara. Gina. Joaquin—seventeen empty beds—Alaina. Meadow. Alex. Carmen. Peter—seventeen reasons to rebel with the hope these will be the last seventeen to be taken by one of three-hundred-ninety-three-million guns in America.

REMEMBERING BOSTON STRONG

Years from now, you'll wish all you remember was
how spring arrived just as you expected, the icicles
gone as magically as they had appeared, the snow
seeped back into the earth, just as you had trusted
it would. The thawed Charles and a river of runners
ribboning that morning through the city that was
a city long before our nation was a nation, while
the ivy scribbled, climbed, turning green the red
bricks your great-great-great grandfathers laid—
memories mortar in every city wall and chimney.

But, years from now, you'll still remember this:
the unexpected smoke that wasn't a spring fog,
pink-purple blossoms mingled with the sparkle
of shattered glass strewn over Boylston Street
bursting red, red maples' tiny leaves opening
like newborn hands to cup April's rain, the lives
of two girls with names as pretty as May flowers,
who would never bloom, the irony of the race
ending with the mangled feet and legs of those
wheeled away by those who did not run away,
and the boy, the son—everyone's son—his life
outlived by the budding tulips of window boxes
dressing-up the city suddenly frozen in spring.

Daylight each day a few minutes longer, but
baseball diamonds dulled and muted, the sky
each day a tint bluer, but stadiums abandoned,
every seat an empty nest. The wind each day
a hint warmer, but park benches cold and quiet,

swings like pendulums—stopped. Each night
crickets louder in your ears, but winter set still
in your eyes caught in the glow of television sets
casting shadows of the news across living rooms
and hollow city streets locked-down in silence.

And years from now, what you'll mostly want
to remember is not the shoot-out that ended
the silent waiting, nor the bombers' names, nor
the blasts, but the tender roses you laid across
the finish line, the thankful praise you gave for
the lives that saved lives in their arms, the brave
promises of those who vowed to walk, dance,
and run again, the stadiums and ballparks again
filled with anthems sung by you, like a thousand
songbirds at once, a chorus into a second spring
you had not expected: dandelions still pushing
through pavement cracks, spiders still spinning,
forsythia still bursting yellow, elms still growing
taller, and ivy still climbing the enduring walls
of the city, still a city, but a whole lot stronger.

AMERICA THE BEAUTIFUL AGAIN

How I sang *O, beautiful* like a psalm at church
with my mother, her Cuban accent scaling-up
every vowel: *O, bee-yoo-tee-ful*, yet in perfect
pitch, delicate and tuned to the radiant beams
of stained glass light. How she taught me to fix
my eyes on the crucifix as we sang our thanks
to our savior for this country that saved us—
our voices hymns as passionate as the organ
piping towards the very heavens. How I sang
for spacious skies closer to those skies while
perched on my father's sun-beat shoulders,
towering above our first Fourth of July parade.
How the timbre through our bodies mingled,
breathing, singing as one with the brass notes
of the marching band playing the only song
he ever learned in English. How I dared sing it
at assembly with my teenage voice cracking
for amber waves of grain that I'd never seen,
nor the *purple mountain majesties*—but could
imagine them in each verse rising from my gut,
every exclamation of praise I belted out until
my throat hurt: *America!* and again *America!*
How I began to read Nietzsche and doubt god,
yet still wished for god to *shed His grace on
thee, and crown thy good with brotherhood.*
How I still want to sing despite all the truth
of our wars and our gunshots ringing louder
than our school bells, our politicians smiling
lies at the mic, the deadlock of our divided

voices shouting over each other instead of
singing together. How I want to sing again—
beautiful or not, just to be harmony—*from
sea to shining sea*—with the only country
I know enough to know how to sing for.

WHAT I KNOW OF COUNTRY

Those picture books from grade-school days:
Pilgrims in tall hats, their gold-buckled shoes
I wanted so badly. White-wigged men standing
tall in velvet-curtained rooms, holding feathers
in their hands, inked words buzzing off the page
into my heart's ear: Life, Liberty, Happiness for
we, the people, singing of shining seas crossed,
the spacious skies of a God-blessed land when
a song and a book were all I knew of country.

I've forgotten the capital of Vermont and Iowa,
but I remember my eyes on a map mesmerized
by faraway cities, towns I couldn't pronounce,
or believe the vast body of this land belonged
to me, and I to it: the Rockies' spine, blue stare
of the Great Lakes, and the endless shoulders
of coastlines, the curvy hips of harbors, rivers
like my palms' lines traced with wonder from
beginning to end, the tiny red dot of my heart
marking where I lived—when what I knew
of country was only what I read from a map.

I wanted to live in the house I dreamed from
television: cushy sofas, crystal candy dishes,
mothers who served perfectly roasted turkeys
with instant stuffing, children with allowances
and perfect teeth, fathers driving teal-blue cars
with silver fins to some country club I'd surely
belong to someday. Though the gunfire, blood

of war beamed into my bedroom, though I fell
asleep, though our men from the moon landed
on my roof with empty promises from space—
fantasy was still all I could believe of country.

I didn't want to change the channel, but I did:
I lifted the shades, let light shine on the carpets
stained with lies I'd missed, and saw the dust
of secrets settled over the photos. The house
began to creak, fall apart around me, alone
for years waiting at the kitchen table, the last
to know, asking my reflection in the windows:
How could you, America? With no answer for
all I knew of country was my hurt and rage.

But home was home: I dusted off the secrets,
cleaned up the lies, nailed the creaky floors
down, set a fire, and sat with history books
I'd never opened, listened to songs I'd never
played, pulled out the old map from a dark
drawer, redrew it with more colors, less lines.
I stoked the fire, burning on until finally: *Okay,
nothing's perfect*, I understood, *I forgive you*,
I said—and forgiveness became my country.

I stayed, you stayed, we stayed for our boys
and girls returning as heroes, some without
legs or arms, for our Challenger and Towers
fainting from the sky, for the terrified lives
of the Big Easy stranded like flightless birds
on roofs, for the sea that drowned our North,

but we swept each grain of sand back to shore,
for the candles we lit for our twenty children
of Sandy Hook, feeling what we've always felt:
to know a country takes all we know of love:

some days better than others, but never easy
to keep our promise every morning of every
year, of every century, and wake up, stumble
downstairs with all our raging hope, sit down
at the kitchen table again, still blurry-eyed,
still tired, and say: *Listen, we need to talk.*

ST. LOUIS: PRAYER AT DAWN

Let the vigil of stars close their weary eyes as we open ours to their brethren, the sun dawning like an answered prayer.

Halleluiah. Let there be light.

One light to breathe color into the black-n-white of St. Louis. Let the stripe down Delmar Boulevard become the seam of a mended city, not remain the tear of a city torn in two—north and south.

Where there is discord, let us bring union. Halleluiah.

Let the northside's gunfire turn into the call of cardinals, again. Let boarded-up windows open, let curtains flutter again with the wind of hope. Let the weeds wither, let abandoned houses bloom into homes with asters and iris. Let there be no southside separate from the north.

You shall not give false testimony against your neighbor.
Halleluiah.

Let us praise our city in common. Let's sit, eat together: the tang of our famous ribs and Provel cheese, the sweet goo of butter cakes.

Halleluiah.

Let's listen, dance together: our Chuck Berry's twang and St. Louis blues down our own Mardi Gras parade.

Halleluiah.

Let's raise our children together: let them ride the same school buses, learn the same history, swing in the same playgrounds, pedal their bikes down the same streets, share their same city.

Then we shall see face to face. Halleluiah.

Let us snuff out the sooty smokestacks. Let sunlight grace every rooftop, every lawn, every backyard, every face down every street. Let the homeless man asleep in Union Station Park rise out of his shadow. Let the windows of office towers reflect the sheen of the Mississippi gleaming with the golden rule:

> *Do unto others as you would have them do unto you.*
> *Halleluiah.*

For cashiers ringing up groceries and jewelers setting diamonds.

> *Love your neighbor as yourself.*

For uniformed bus drivers and tycoons suited in their boardrooms.

> *Love your neighbor as yourself.*

For mothers kissing their sons and daughters goodbye at daycare, and mothers at home baking cupcakes with them.

> *Love your neighbor as yourself. Halleluiah.*

Let there be love. Let us believe these words:

> *Faith, hope, and love. But the greatest of these is love.*
> *Love never fails.*

Let the steel arch bend into the shape of a heart—brilliant, strong, constant. Let love be our gateway.

> *Halleluiah. Let there be light.*

NOW WITHOUT ME

Now that my brow is as creased as my palms,
now that I am imagining my home without
me, now that I ponder the someday when I
and my hands will no longer be here needed
to till the soil of my iris beds. Now that I know
they'll bloom like sapphires without my eyes
to praise them, or to wink back at the wings
of butterflies. Now that the lavender will still
perfume the breeze without my inhale, and
the ivy will scrawl without my pruning. Now
that chipmunks won't need my ears to hear
them chirp as they dart-and-dash, content
as children at play unaware of their mortality.

My father died at fifty-five. I'm fifty, supposing
I might only have five years left to breathe-in
the pine-scented breeze scaling up my hillside,
five years' worth of languid hours on my porch
with my cat, five years to ask why, despite a life
spent believing nothing but *this* life, now I want
to believe there's some god that only my pulse
explains in sync—not only with this here/now—
but with all I am from: my mother's lavish black
hair and sorrows, my father's immense silence,
my grandmother's scolding that I crafted into
a wisdom still guiding me like the aglow embers
of my grandfather's cigar, the iron-red memory
of his Cuban mountains he never beheld again.

To believe I didn't begin with *me*, nor will end
with *me*, never been a *me*, but a soul beyond
clinging to any home or country—a larger part
of a continuum in the amber light of each dawn
that powders my face and the drifting gestures
of clouds alluding to the first time we assumed
the sun's power with spark of flint on dry brush
to kindle our own flames. That this very poem
from my hands owes itself to the hands that first
mixed soot and tallow with imagination to draw
myth across their cave walls, and to the throats
that first tamed grunts into breaths of language,
gave meaning to the toil of spear and slaughter.

The cosmos may well be a chance clash of rock,
a callous dust, but now that sometimes I forget
names and days of the week, I want to believe
all my endeavors as willed by an eternal desire
held in the wide-open arms of the Milky Way
and in the voice of these lines as consequence,
as witness, ages from now for others to adore
as I have adored: fireflies like constellations,
moonlight shadows like showers, lark songs
like thunder. Lose as I've gladly lost my desire
to name everything or belong to anything but
myself amid my birches bending in the wind.
Imagine as I've imagined: life beyond my bones
that now ache with rain, and relinquish me.

AND SO WE ALL FALL DOWN

{after and for Anselm Kiefer's installation:
Steigend steigend sinke nieder
(rising, rising, falling down), 2009–2012}

And so the hunks of pavement heaved and set
before us are every road we've tired, and those
we wish we had, and those we will, and those
we never will, or those that'll dead-end when
our empire ends. And so let our debris to be
reassembled as tenderly as these curated bits
of rubble letting us see how chaos yields order,
and order chaos. And so let our nation's faces
be these boulders like tiny, bruised moons out
of orbit, and yet enduring, still spinning across
the shiny gallery floor, despite the brutal love
of the universe and brutal love for our country.
And so let us believe we won't simply end like
the speck of a star that will explode as quietly
as a poem whispered above our rooftops into
a black hole into the black night. And so let us
believe there is still eternity even in our ruin,
like this art made out of these remains, made
more alive by destruction. And so all the dead
stalks of these sunflowers embalmed with paint
and fixed by our imagination dangling forever
from the ceiling like acrobats that'll never fall.
And so the hope in what they let us hope: that
our ideals won't all disappear, that some trace
of what we have believed must endure beyond
our decay, beyond entropy's law, assuring us
we'll live on, even after our inevitable dissolve.

CLOUD ANTHEM

Until we are clouds that tear like bread but
mend like bones. Until we weave each other
like silk sheets shrouding mountains, or bear
gales that shear us. Until we soften our hard
edges, free to become any shape imaginable:
a rose or an angel crafted by the breeze like
papier-mâché or a lion or dragon like marble
chiseled by gusts. Until we scatter ourselves—
pebbles of grey puffs, but then band together
like stringed pearls. Until we learn to listen to
each other, as thunderous as opera or as soft
as a showered lullaby. Until we truly treasure
the sunset, lavish it in mauve, rust, and rose.
Until we have the courage to vanish like sails
into the horizon, or be at peace, anchored still.
Until we move without any measure, as vast
as continents or as petite as islands, floating
in an abyss of virtual blue we belong to. Until
we dance tango with the moon and comfort
the jealous stars, falling. Until we care enough
for the earth to bless it as morning fog. Until
we realize we're muddy as puddles, pristine
as lakes not yet clouds. Until we remember
we're born from rivers and dewdrops. Until
we are at ease to dissolve as wispy showers,
not always needing to clash like godly yells
of thunder. Until we believe lightning roots
are not our right to the ground. Though we
collude into storms that ravage, we can also
sprinkle ourselves like memories. Until we

tame the riot of our tornadoes, settle down
into a soft drizzle, into a daydream. Though
we may curse with hail, we can absolve with
snowflakes. We can die valiant as rainbows,
and hold light in our lucid bodies like blood.
We can decide to move boundlessly, without
creed or desire. Until we are clouds meshed
within clouds sharing a kingdom with no king,
a city with no walls, a country with no name,
a nation without any borders or claim. Until
we abide as one together in one single sky.

AUTHOR'S NOTE

Over six years ago, as I waited to be called up to the podium before the National Mall to recite the occasional poem I had written for President Obama's second inaugural ceremony, I remember turning to my mother and whispering, "*Mamá*, I think we're finally *americanos*." That indelible moment and my experiences as the first Latinx, immigrant, and gay man to serve as Presidential Inaugural Poet set a newfound place for me at the proverbial American table, one that I had not expected. Indeed, I came to definitively understand and believe that my story—alongside the stories of millions like me from marginalized walks of life—is, and has always been, a grand part of our country's cultural and historical narrative. Granted, it's a part that has witnessed outright discrimination and oppression, and has been scarcely acknowledged and barely honored. But it's also one that has been, and continues to steadily be, written into the work-in-progress that is our nation, thanks largely to the fortitude of the many artists, activists, writers, leaders, and trailblazers on many fronts who have strived and continue striving to give voice to the marginalized and to generate dialogue with those who marginalize. In this regard, the public role I was assigned as inaugural poet prompted me to explore more deeply my own civic and artistic duty in questioning and contributing to the American narrative through my poetry and the capacity of the genre itself to foster understanding and offer new perspectives.

This collection is largely the culmination of that deeper exploration. The title, *How to Love a Country*, is both a statement of hope in our nationhood and an implied question about our struggles with it. My intent was to ground these poems in the complexity and contradictions of my personal, as well as our collective, relationship to our country, given the many sociopolitical issues that remain unresolved: immigration, gender, race, and sexuality, among others. Thematically and emotionally, the poems aspire to have a conversation, not only with myself, not only with other poets and artists, but also with all Americans, from our past and present, through an oracular yet intimate *village voice* that speaks to matters that continue to concern and affect us en masse: Poetry indebted to our pantheon of visionaries, such as Martin Luther King Jr., Rosa Parks, Gloria Steinem, and Cesar Chávez, as well as our musical folk heroes, such as Joan Baez and Bob Dylan. Poetry equally inspired by everyday Americans, like my mother, who maintains her faith in our country's promises yet also holds it accountable. Poetry informed by the tradition and spirit of predecessors such as Walt Whitman, Langston Hughes, James Baldwin, Allen Ginsberg, Adrienne Rich, Gloria Anzaldúa, Joy Harjo, Sandra Cisneros, Jimmy Santiago Baca, and Martín Espada, as well as the current chorus of socially conscious poetry that actively responds to the most pressing concerns of our day.

In that respect, and in alignment with the intention of this collection, I included several occasional or commissioned poems that I've written over the last few years. I'm fascinated by both the challenges these types of poems present and the dynamics they represent: how such poems must—and can—occupy public space, engage an audience in real, live social settings, and echo the oral tradition of poetry as storytelling, the proverbial village gathered around the proverbial campfire to celebrate, advocate, debate, and grieve together as cultural co-agents through poetry. Such was my experience with poems like "Until We Could," written to champion the cause of marriage equality; "Remembering Boston Strong" and "One Pulse—One Poem," written to honor the victims and survivors of the Boston Marathon bombings and the Pulse nightclub shooting, respectively; and "St. Louis: Prayer Before Dawn," which addressed the racial and class divide of the city. In this vein, I also included poems that originally appeared in *Boundaries*, a limited-edition fine-press book in collaboration with the photographer Jacob Hessler. These poems challenge the physical, imagined, and psychological dividing lines—both historic and current—that shadow America and perpetuate an *us* vs. *them* mind-set by inciting irrational fears, hate, and prejudice, as opposed to our hopes and ideals of indeed becoming a *boundaryless* nation.

In contrast to these more civic-minded and socially engaged poems, I wove into the collection more personal, autobiographical poems to add dimension and complexity to the aforementioned themes and concerns through a more private, tighter lens. I intended the contrast to create a kind of dialogue between the poetry of the "I" and the poetry of the "we": The poem "Matters of the Sea," an occasional written for the reopening of the US Embassy in Havana, in contrast to "My Father in English," which narrates my father's struggles as an exile. Or "Easy Lynching on Herndon Avenue," a poem regarding the last recorded lynching in the US, in contrast to *"El Americano* in the Mirror," which exposes my own retaliatory biases and prejudices. These contrasts were also meant to reflect the essential beauty and constant struggle of our democracy as expressed in our nation's motto: *e pluribus unum* (*out of many, one*). We are a populace of individual "I's" who have consented to come together as a "we." The challenge has been to continuously question who is (or isn't) included in that "we" and how to redefine and reimagine it.

Overall, we've managed to move toward a more inclusive under-standing of ourselves and acceptance of each other. Historically, though, we have wavered and are currently at a crossroads: Are we going to advance toward a broader definition of "we" or will we retreat to a narrower one? That is essentially the question—with all its hopes and fears—that is at the heart of this collection, both personally and collectively.

As Roque Dalton wrote, "Poetry, like bread, is for everyone." My tenure as inaugural poet has reaffirmed my belief in those words, which I continue to champion on many fronts. In addition to writing the poems in this collection, which I hope are indeed *like bread*, I continue to crisscross the nation in order to bring po-etry to such unlikely venues as the Federal Reserve, engineering and law firms, the Mayo Clinic, and the US Department of Agri-culture, as well as to support advocacy groups of all kinds: immi-gration reform, LGBTQ rights and youth, and anti–gun violence groups, among others. Believing that poetry can indeed change lives, which can in turn change the world, I partnered with the Academy of American Poets as their first-ever Education Ambas-sador, assisting in the development and distribution of resources that help teachers more effectively bring the life-enriching power of poetry into classrooms. As visiting professor at Florida Interna-tional University and Colby College, I developed courses on the intersectionality of poetry, art, and community to engage stu-dents through the public humanities. And in collaboration with Boston public radio station WGBH, I created *The Village Voice*, a segment that discusses poetry's relevance to current events. As a child from an immigrant, working-class family, I was essentially denied poetry; all these efforts are an attempt to counteract that experience by advocating for more generous and meaningful ac-cess to poetry for everybody.

. . .

I give thanks that the figurative stars of all my endeavors
have aligned to create this collection, which I hope conveys
my belief in the agency that poetry can awaken in us and the
power of our shared humanity. For readers who might want
more backstory, historical references, anecdotes, or insights
on some of the poems, I offer the following notes:

"Como Tú / *Like You* / *Like Me*" is dedicated to the young
people impacted by DACA and the DREAMAct, who
are often called *DREAMers*. DACA refers to the Deferred
Action for Childhood Arrivals, an American immigration
policy that allows some individuals who were brought to
the United States illegally as children to receive a renew-
able two-year period of deferred action from deportation.
The DREAM Act (short for Development, Relief, and
Education for Alien Minors Act) was a bill in Congress that
would have granted legal status to certain undocumented
immigrants who were brought to the United States as
children and went to school here. Although several ver-
sions of the bill have been introduced in Congress since
2001, it has never passed.

"Staring at Aspens: A History Lesson" was prompted by a present-
day photo of the Navajo Nation and based on research into
the Long Walk of the Navajo, when 8,500 Navajos (from 1864
through 1866) were forced to walk nearly three hundred miles
from their traditional lands in the eastern Arizona Territory
and western New Mexico Territory to Fort Sumner (in an
area called the Bosque Redondo or *Hwééldi* by the Navajo).
They were held captive there until 1868, when they were
released and allowed to return to their ancestral homelands,

known as the "Long Walk" home. The poem first appeared in the limited-edition collection *Boundaries* and has been slightly revised for this volume.

"Letter from Yi Cheung." Known as the "Ellis Island of the West," Angel Island served as an immigration station from 1910 to 1940, processing approximately 175,000 Chinese immigrants. However, unlike with the processing of immigrants at Ellis Island, Chinese immigrants were often detained for months, subjected to humiliating medical examinations, and interrogated to prove they had husbands or fathers who were US citizens or else face deportation, due to the Chinese Exclusion Act of 1882. After much factual research and emotional surveying of many Chinese immigration stories from Angel Island, I made the artistic choice to write a persona poem, not to appropriate those stories but as the most authentic and visceral way the genre could honor those stories and bring them to life for the reader. The poem first appeared in the limited-edition collection *Boundaries* and has been slightly revised for this volume.

"Leaving in the Rain: Limerick, Ireland" (originally titled "Leaving Limerick in the Rain: A Letter to Ireland") first appeared in *Liberation: New Works on Freedom from Internationally Renowned Poets* (Beacon Press, 2015), edited by Mark Ludwig.

"Matters of the Sea" was commissioned by the US Department of State to commemorate the reopening of the US Embassy in Havana, Cuba, where I recited the poem during the ceremony on August 14, 2015. The poem was published in chapbook form as a bilingual edition with translation

into Spanish by Ruth Behar. It is one of the most emotionally complex poems I've ever written, invested with my love for the people of two countries that are part of my very being. While politics may sometimes divide people, I believe the deep attachments to family, country, and the memory of home have the capacity to bring us together. In that respect, the poem aims to evoke our shared humanity and humbly serve as a catalyst for meaningful changes in Cuba and a new understanding among Cubans everywhere.

"Island Body" was commissioned by Bacardi Limited and served as the script for a short film and radio segment. While this was a more commercial commission, as a Cuban American I obviously felt personally drawn to the plight of exiles like the Arechabala family (originators of Havana Club rum), who were forced to flee Cuba at gunpoint. The poem has been slightly revised for this volume.

"Mother Country": When the White House asked me to serve as Presidential Inaugural Poet for Barack Obama, they requested that I submit three original poems for their consideration. "Mother Country" was the third poem I wrote. It appeared in my memoir *For All of Us, One Today: An Inaugural Poet's Journey* (Beacon Press).

"Easy Lynching on Herndon Avenue" makes reference to a present-day photo at the site of the last recorded lynching (by hanging) in the United States. It is of interest to note that a lawsuit was filed at the request of Michael Donald's mother, Beulah Mae Donald. The Ku Klux Klan was found civilly liable; the settlement bankrupted the United Klans of America and

became a precedent for civil legal action against other racist hate groups. The poem first appeared in the limited-edition collection *Boundaries*.

"Poetry Assignment #4: What Do You Miss Most?": In 2005 I taught creative writing at Arlington Correctional Facility through a program developed and administered by Georgetown University, where I also served as an English instructor. The "poem" embedded within this poem is not a verbatim transcript but, rather, a recollection of the various poems one particular inmate ("Germaine") wrote throughout the semester, as well as the stories he shared with me, which proved to be one of the most enlightening and rewarding experiences I've ever had as a teacher. He was quite a talented writer, and this poem is intended as a tribute to his talent and his life's journey, as well as to call out the injustices of the racially biased institutions of incarceration in the US.

"St. Louis: Prayer Before Dawn" and *"St. Louis: Prayer at Dawn"* were commissioned by St. Art, a poetry and street-art festival created to stimulate a dialogue to overcome the socioeconomic and racial barriers of St. Louis through the creative and transformative process of art.

"Until We Could" was commissioned to commemorate and celebrate the tenth anniversary of Freedom to Marry, the organization that developed the leading national strategy for marriage equality in the US. The poem is dedicated to Mark Neveu and our journey together for over twenty years. A short film of the poem was produced by Peter Spears and narrated by Ben Forster and Robin Wright. The poem has been slightly revised for this volume.

"*One Pulse—One Poem*" was written in response to the Pulse nightclub shooting of June 12, 2016. The tragedy particularly disturbed and affected me as a gay man, who understands that places like Pulse are not merely nightclubs; they are community; they are a surrogate home for many like me. To have such a home desecrated in such a manner was doubly devastating. In that respect, I intended for the poem to speak of the very act of writing a poem as a way to process our shared grief and honor the lives of the victims and survivors. The poem appeared in *Bullets into Bells: Poets & Citizens Respond to Gun Violence*, a powerful anthology that brings together the voices of poets and citizens most impacted to call for the end of gun violence with the activist power of poetry. "One Pulse—One Poem" was first published in the *Miami Herald*.

"*Remembering Boston Strong*" was written in response to the Boston Marathon bombings of April 15, 2013, and the harrowing days that followed, but, more importantly, in remembrance of the victims and in celebration of the resiliency of the survivors and Boston's denizens. The poem was published in chapbook form and also recorded at the Boston Strong benefit concert. Net proceeds from the sale of the chapbook and CD benefit the One Fund Boston, the main charitable effort for donations supporting bombing victims and their families.

"*What I Know of Country*": When the White House asked me to serve as Presidential Inaugural Poet for Barack Obama, they requested that I submit three original poems for their consideration. "What I Know of Country" was the first poem I wrote. This poem also appeared in my memoir *For All of Us, One Today: An Inaugural Poet's Journey*.

"*And So We All Fall Down*" is a quasi-ekphrastic poem reflecting on Anselm Kiefer's *Steigend steigend sinke nieder (rising, rising, falling down)* 2009–2012 large-scale installation, an assembly of debris collected from the demolition of the Rue des Archives in Paris.

The **Adrienne Rich** quote that appears as an epigraph is from a piece by Rich, "Legislators of the World," from the *Guardian*, November 18, 2006. The **James Baldwin** quote as epigraph is from "*The Black Scholar* Interviews James Baldwin, in *Conversations with James Baldwin*, edited by Fred L. Standley and Louis H. Pratt (University Press of Mississippi, 1989).

ACKNOWLEDGMENTS

Though the act of writing is a solitary one, *being* a writer involves being part of communities that allow one to thrive through camaraderie and friendship. In that regard, I'm indebted and forever grateful to my friends, fellow writers, and readers who helped me shape this collection: Kim Dower, Brian Leung, Caridad Moro-Gronlier, and Nikki Moustaki; and to my partner, Mark Neveu, for his patience at the kitchen table going over every poem together. I'm equally grateful to the founders and directors of Two Ponds Press, Ken Shure and Liv Rockefeller, for their vision of *Boundaries*, a gorgeous limited-edition collection in which several of the poems in this volume first appeared, with Jacob Hessler's brilliant photography. As such, my awe and thanks to Jacob for his talents and artistic eye, which inspired and prompted those poems, and to Alissa Morris, who guided us both through the whole endeavor. I praise the many organizations and institutions that commissioned some of the poems in this collection for their respect and belief in the power of poetry to speak to a broad human experience beyond the page. Finally, Helene Atwan, director of my essential community at Beacon Press, which shares my same values and commitment to poetry and its role in shaping a more equitable and truthful world.

ABOUT THE AUTHOR

Selected by Barack Obama as the fifth Presidential Inaugural Poet in US history, Richard Blanco stands as the youngest and the first Latinx, immigrant, and gay person to serve in such a role. Born in Madrid to Cuban exile parents and raised in Miami, he focuses on the negotiation of cultural identity and universal themes of place and belonging in both his body of work and his advocacy.

Blanco is the author of the poetry collections *Looking for the Gulf Motel*, *Directions to the Beach of the Dead*, and *City of a Hundred Fires*; the memoirs *The Prince of Los Cocuyos: A Miami Childhood* and *For All of Us, One Today: An Inaugural Poet's Journey*; a children's edition of his presidential inaugural poem, "One Today," illustrated by Dav Pilkey; and *Boundaries*, a collaboration with photographer Jacob Hessler. In addition, Blanco has written and performed occasional poems for organizations and events such as the re-opening of the US embassy in Cuba, the Boston Strong Benefit Concert, and Freedom to Marry. His poems and essays have appeared in various publications, such as the *New Yorker*, the *Best American Poetry* series, the *Nation*, *New Republic*, *Huffington Post*, and *Condé Nast Traveler*. Currently, he is the contributing poet to "The Village Voice," a bimonthly segment on Boston public radio station WGBH, which discusses news topics through the lens of socially conscious poetry.

Blanco has received numerous honorary degrees and literary awards, including the Agnes Lynch Starrett Poetry Prize from the University of Pittsburgh Press, the Pen/Beyond Margins Award, the Paterson Poetry Prize, two Maine Literary Awards, the Thom Gunn Award, and a Lambda Literary Award. He is a fellow of the Bread Loaf Writers' Conference and a Woodrow Wilson Visiting Fellow, and has taught at Wesleyan University, Georgetown University, American University, Colby College, and Florida International University. He currently serves as the first-ever Education Ambassador for the Academy of American Poets and is a member of the Obama Foundation's advisory council.